A GATHERING
OF
DOVES

DORIS M. DAY

SAMUEL  FRENCH

LONDON
NEW YORK TORONTO SYDNEY HOLLYWOOD

CHARACTERS:

THE BLUES
Ellen White
her daughter-in-law
Mary White
Celia White
Ellen's young daughter

THE REDS
Gran Black
Tottie Black
her middle-aged daughter
Edna
Tottie's daughter
Wyn Green

The action passes in a living-room of an ordinary family, in a country torn by civil war

Time – the present

PRODUCER'S NOTE

While it is obvious that the play is based on the situation in Ireland, it is deliberately set in an anonymous country, for it is a situation that is paralleled wherever civil strife separates friend and family. The women are real characters, and should not in any way be overdramatized. The situation is real enough—for such is life . . .

A GATHERING OF DOVES

SCENE 1

Introductory music: "Mars—God of War": The Planets Suite (Holst)

The living-room of an ordinary family, in a country torn by civil war. Early morning

The furniture shows signs of wear, and there is a general air of untidiness and unrest. The window is partially boarded up where the glass has been broken, and the curtains are torn in one or two places. A door leads to the kitchen and another to the hall and front door. A settee, rather broken down, is obviously used as a makeshift bed. Clothes are thrown over the back of an armchair, and a table shows evidence of a hastily snatched meal

When the play begins the room is in darkness, though daylight is beginning to seep through the shutters at the back. The only sound is of broken glass being swept up outside, and the general noises as a city gathers its resources after a night of battle. Mrs Black (Tottie) is asleep on the settee. She is middle-aged, tired and perplexed. Gran, her mother, comes downstairs and enters the room from the hall. She is an elderly woman who has seen the troubles of the world and has learnt to cope with them. She is fairly agile for her age and should not in any way be caricatured as an old lady in her dotage. She is experienced enough to accept life with all its tragedies, etc., and is a very practical person. She gently pulls the curtains and then carefully takes down a shutter or two. This is not enough to show much of the street outside, but it does reveal a broken window and a patch of clear sky. She looks at Tottie, then turns again and stares out at the street

Edna enters from the hall. She is Tottie's daughter, in her early thirties, and still has a lot of fight in her. She has a bandaged head and looks dirty and dishevelled. She is wearing slacks, etc.

Gran You out again last night?

Edna No. I was stretched out in front of a lovely fire wearing a purple négligé and sipping champagne during the commercials on television.

Gran Sarcasm won't get you anywhere, my girl. What you done to your head?

Edna I copped a brick. It's a bloody wonder I didn't lose my eye.

Gran You never used to swear.

Edna I never used to watch my man throwing petrol bombs half the night. (*She looks at Tottie*) Mum's well away—she looks whacked—why isn't she in bed?

Gran Your aunt wanted help with young Chrissie. She started her pains just after you left—had a boy early this morning.

Edna Christ! There was a right battle over that way, too—fancy having a baby in the middle of that.

Gran You were born in the middle of an air-raid—you've survived.

Edna To fight another war . . .

Gran There's always been wars, of one sort or another.

Edna (*bitterly*) The cry of wisdom. Any chance of a cup of tea?

Gran If there's any gas. If not we'll have to get the fire going again.

Gran exits to the kitchen

Edna kneels before the fire and as she kneels, she winces and holds her head. The hopelessness of the situation is in her face, but she gathers her spirit and begins to stoke the fire, raking it out, etc., till a glow begins to show. The sound wakens Tottie, but Edna takes no notice of her till she sits up and hunts around for her shoes. Tottie notices the bandage

Tottie You've hurt your head. (*It is an acceptance of fact rather than a shock*)

Edna It was only a brick—it could have been a bullet.

Tottie Did the barricades come down across the Square?

Edna Yes, but no doubt they're up again somewhere else.

Gran enters with a bottle in time to hear the last remark

Gran Win one, lose one—who wins in the end? (*She begins to pour milk from a bottle into the cups*)

Tottie Where's the jug?

Gran I didn't look for it.

Tottie (*snapping*) We're not in the gutter yet . . . go and look for it.

Gran Is that a request, madam—or an order?

Edna I'll go.

Edna exits to the kitchen

Tottie It's bad enough out there—we don't have to live like pigs in here.

Gran You call this living? Milk in a bottle is a damn sight better than petrol. That's the last of it any rate—and that's not too fresh.

Edna enters with a jug

Tottie I wonder why they didn't deliver yesterday.

Gran No doubt someone blew up the cow.

Edna That's stupid talk, Gran.

Gran There's dafter things than that being done in this place— and all in the name of fair play, too . . .

Tottie If he doesn't come today we'll have to use dried milk. It won't do us any harm.

Gran You can drink it if you like, but I'm not. I'll get my old bike out and ride down to see young James. He'll not grudge me a drop of milk.

Edna I believe you would and all!

Gran Why not? I'll put up with a lot—clear up the mess and the dust from the explosions and sleep in a chair if necessary, but God help me if I've got to sup some manufactured rubbish before I can drink a decent cup of tea . . .

There is a commotion as someone enters through the front door. Tottie moves towards the hall door

Wyn Green enters. She is middle-aged, intelligent. She has been a bit of a firebrand, but it is beginning to dampen. At the moment she is dirty and walks with a heavy limp, collapsing into the armchair

Wyn The Blues lobbed a petrol bomb. George had just parked his car and the whole bloody lot went up . . .

Tottie George?

Wyn No-one could get near—even Heidi—and she tried hard enough, poor bitch . . .

Gran Heidi, too. How he loved that little dog . . .

Edna Is she all right?

Wyn She was burnt alive—her coat caught fire . . .

Edna What about the others? Nell? Alan?

Wyn They're O.K. We all dived out the back as the front caved in. They're a bit bruised and battered. Alan split the seat of his trousers.

Edna He always was a bit behind. (*It is a bitter joke*)

Wyn He had on the most ridiculous flowered pants. (*She starts to giggle, but it starts to become hysterical*)

Tottie (*shouting at her*) Shut up! Shut up!!

A silence follows. Gran collects her coat from the back of the armchair

Where're you going, Mum?

Gran Someone's got to go and tell Jean—she'll be waiting for George to come home——

Edna —and the baby due soon . . .

Tottie Have your tea first, Mum.

Gran I couldn't touch it.

Gran exits to the hall

Wyn She shouldn't be the one to go.

Tottie Let her. She's seen so much, and known so much of her own sorrow. She's the one to help Jean—if anyone can.

Edna What do you say, for Christ's sake?

Tottie What do you say? "I'm sorry, Jean, but your baby won't have a father. Someone—no-one you know—and no doubt, someone who didn't know you, decided to throw a petrol bomb, and I'm afraid that it hit George's car. He was burnt alive, Jean. No-one can help him—he just burnt—like a roast pig—and incidentally, Jean—your pet dog died, too. I'm sorry, Jean, but that's life! Of course, if there's anything we can do

—don't hesitate to ask!" That's what you say, girl, and a fat lot of help it is, too . . .

Wyn It's time we helped ourselves. We've all had enough. We've seen death, and our homes destroyed, and for what? Because some of our forefathers fought under a Blue flag and some the Red—because we support the arguments and principles of something that divided us hundreds of years ago.

Edna Aren't the principles worth supporting?

Wyn Principles that divide brother from brother, children from parents—that maim and kill? That bring foreign soldiers into our country to keep us apart?

Edna You've changed your tune. You were the one who rallied us to help the cause. There's some who would call you a traitor.

Tottie I wouldn't. The only cause I want to support right now is the right to live decently. (*She looks round the room in disgust*) It doesn't worry me if some think differently, let them—and let us have some peace.

Edna You can't say that, Mum. Look at the killing—think of George—are you going to let the bastards that did that get away scot free?

Tottie Since when have *our* men been plaster saints? Or you either, for that matter? I don't care a damn who is right and who is wrong—enough is enough . . .

Wyn We're not getting anywhere—we kill two of theirs, blow up their houses, and they do the same to us. We've just got to call a halt before the whole bloody lot goes up and there's nothing left; nobody worth saving. You say I've changed my tune, but it's not been an overnight change, though George being killed like that, just about finished me.

Edna Why George? There have been plenty of others.

Tottie Too many.

Wyn (*as if in a dream*) Last night—looking over the barricades before that car blew up—I saw Mary White . . .

Edna So?

Wyn She was one of the first children I ever taught—a bright lovable girl—she spent half her time helping others—she couldn't bear to see anyone hurt . . .

Edna (*sarcastically*) That's a weakness she's obviously overcome.

Tottie She's had reason. Her Tom was killed when our boys blew up the police station in March. Before she married him, she was head over heels in love with George—or so we thought, but she never had eyes for anyone else once Tom came on the scene.

Edna George wouldn't have married one of *them*.

Tottie You knew nothing, Edna. You were abroad. Did you think twice before you married Franz? He was an alien to us, remember.

Edna It wasn't the same.

Tottie Of course it was. It wasn't twenty years before that that *your* father was fighting *his* father. Yes, and fought alongside the Blue Bannermen. It's only in the last few years that agitators have decided to stir things up and divide us with tales of old hatreds.

Wyn Don't you want to see your children home again, and living without fear of a walk down the street?

Edna Even if I did—and I do—the men won't give way.

Wyn Then we must make them.

Edna We'd be banging our heads against the brick wall.

Wyn Then we keep on banging until we make them see sense.

Edna It won't work and you know it. I don't care if Mary White was an angel once. The Blues are devils now, the whole shooting match of them. No respecters of hair or hide. Look at what they did to young Chrissie. Beat her up black and blue, and then raped her for good measure. She's never been the same since—nigh on lost her reason. And now she's got a son —what's going to happen to that poor little bastard?

Tottie Are we any better when we stand by and let our men maim and kill? We do, you know. Every time we fill a bottle with petrol or build a barricade, someone gets hurt, someone's killed.

Edna We've got to protect our own.

Wyn From what? Who? It's not a foreign power that's invaded us. We're fighting our own countrymen.

Edna Then they don't deserve the name—and nor will you—I reckon you've gone out of your senses.

Wyn No. I've just come to them.

Edna If we give in now, the Blues will dominate this country. They'll control the jobs, the housing, the whole economy and we'll be left to struggle with what's left.

Tottie And if we beat them—we'll do the same.

Edna We'll do it a damn sight more democratically and fairly than they will.

Wyn Will we? Who do we mean by "we", any rate? It won't be the likes of us that'll be ruling—don't kid yourself. It will be the leaders, the politically minded bureaucrats—and in the end, they'll either have to negotiate with the other side, or destroy them all. Would you want that?

Edna They'll never agree.

Wyn It's domination of one side or another. One side wins, another loses. One side on top, and the others under an iron rule. Do you want that? A totalitarian state? Or do you want democracy—shaky and imperfect as it might be?

Tottie There's not much choice, is there?

Wyn Is there ever? But we've got to call a halt to this fighting, destroying. There's no sanity, no reason—it's madness and you know it.

Tottie She's right, Edna. There must be an end somewhere, and please God—this can't be it—not this mess.

Wyn Edna. You used to work with Mary before you went abroad, didn't you?

Edna What of it?

Wyn I know Mary. She hasn't changed that much, and I saw the mood she was in last night. As sick as I was. I feel that if we can contact her and find others of similar attitudes, we may be able to have a get-together and see if this is the end, or if we can find a way to put paid to this misery.

Tottie We could never get past the barricades—they'd lynch us,

Wyn There are ways and means. We can rally our own women. but we must have co-operation from the Blues—otherwise we're lost before we start.

Edna I haven't talked to Mary for years.

Wyn Then the sooner you start the better. I'd go, but it needs someone agile, and since last night, I'm certainly not that.

Tottie Your leg—I forget—come and sit here, and I'll clean it up for you.

Tottie helps Wyn to the sofa, then exits to the kitchen

Edna Your leg—my head. We're a bright pair.

Wyn Pin pricks, when you compare them to the other casualties of the night. Now. You know that our boys are building up to a big offensive attack. But the soldiers are moving in. They're bringing up their armoured cars across the Square—it'll be sheer murder. No-one will gain, even the soldiers—they'll be like piggy in the middle, being fired at from all sides.

Edna That'll teach them to keep their noses out of other people's business.

Wyn Don't be so blind. Do you think that they want to be there? They are doing a police job—trying to separate two hotheads who can't see sense.

Edna You've got it all pat, haven't you?

Wyn I've had time. Sitting beside what was left of George and Heidi for the last six hours.

Tottie returns from the kitchen with a bowl of hot water and some sheeting. During the ensuing dialogue, she washes the wound on Wyn's leg, cutting away the cloth to get to it, and tearing the sheets into strips for bandages

I've made a few contacts, too, before I came here. Someone is expected to deliver a message some time today. Will you be the one?

Edna (*warily*) And if I agree—where do I go?

Wyn Go over to Lacey's—that warehouse on Brice Street—ask for Jean, she works in the canteen.

Edna That's the ginger-headed woman who's got a twisted arm, isn't it?

Wyn She was injured when she was a young girl—another uprising. Now, tell her you've come for the empties, and then ask her for the boxes—the Green ones. She'll understand and will take you into the yard at the back. Stay there by the packing cases, until you see a *green* rug being shaken out of the window of the houses that back on to the yard. It should be hanging there already, but don't make a move till someone actually *shakes* it. Then climb to the roof of the shed, and drop into the garden at the back.

Edna And then what?

Wyn Hide in the privy, till someone fetches you.

Edna Suppose I walk into a trap? I've got that I don't trust anyone.

Wyn You've got to have some trust. I've done all I can, and as far as I know, my contacts are sound.

Edna What do you think, Mum?

Tottie I don't think any more. I live from day to day. It was the same for your Gran during the last troubles. We struggle on, doing the best we can. But I don't want you hurt, love.

Edna During the last war, you drove an ambulance, didn't you?

Tottie Yes.

Edna You always hated the sight of blood. I remember you saying how sick you used to be after a heavy night, picking up the casualties. Why didn't you find another job, Mum? Some job where you didn't have to handle the air-raid victims?

Tottie I never gave it a thought—it had to be done by someone . . .

The Lights fade as Wyn and Doris both look at Edna

SCENE 2

The same. Later that evening

The shutters are up at the window again. The table has been cleared and the room generally tidied—also the occupants. Tottie is sitting on the settee, but is not settled. Gran is sitting in the armchair opposite, mending a pair of trousers

Gran Did you tell Jack?

Tottie He'd have blasted me off the ground . . .

Gran He used to be the peaceful one.

Tottie Not now.

Gran Being out of work for so long has warped his sense of proportion. I never thought he could be so bitter.

Tottie When they closed the yards, they closed his smile.

Gran I don't know what he would have done without the little you brought in.

Tottie It's not been an easy time for any of us . . . but it was a damn sight better before this last strife set in. It's broken Jack. He's more used to making bricks than breaking them.

The two women sit in thought. There is a burst of gunfire

I wish Edna would come in.

Gran She'll have gone home first. Otherwise Franz would have come looking for her. She'll be down as soon as she gets the chance.

The sound of street warfare continues, and ebbs and flows throughout the scene

Tottie It's the waiting that gets you down. I've been worrying all day. When I went back to see young Chrissie I nearly told the others about Edna, but I thought it best not to. There were several of the neighbours in—looking at the baby.

Gran Looking to see what colour he was, I suppose.

Tottie He's white, but he's a scraggy little thing.

Gran He's a baby. That's all that matters, and he'll need a bit more loving than most, having a near demented mother and a bastard for a father.

Tottie That's the first time I've heard you swear, Mum.

Gran Then I'm in the fashion—any rate, decent words are too good for the man that begat that child and drove Chrissie to the state she's in.

Tottie She was quieter today than I've seen her for a long time. Like a child playing with a new toy—oblivious of anyone else.

Gran She'll have to be watched.

There is silence for a while, and then Tottie absent-mindedly starts humming a tune—realizes its significance and smiles

Tottie Funny how a tune sticks. I've had that running round my head all day. It must be years since I heard it. You used to sing it when I was small . . .

Gran And it always made you cry . . . (*She takes up the song shakily at first*)
"God bless my soldier Daddy, to war he's had to go.
Protect him from all danger, because I love him so.
Take care of him when fighting, don't let me pray in vain.
God bless my soldier Daddy, and bring him safe home again."† (*There is a short pause*) He never did come home, though . . .

Tottie I reckon you had a bellyful, one way and another.

† *See page 25 for Music*

Gran Oh. We've had our share of happy times, it's just that at times like this you're apt to forget them. I remember that when your dad and I got married we never had two pennies to rub together—we went up to the park for a picnic—that was our honeymoon, and then back to our own home. One room at the top of an old tenement, with a lav in the garden and a tap on the landing—all shared with the other tenants. But that room was ours, and every stick in it paid for and kept clean and bright. Mind you, being upstairs meant that we got all the smells—always knew what everyone in the house was eating. Cabbage, fish—the lot. I remember one day there was a terrible smell, and the place was filled with smoke—enough to turn over your stomach. I went down to see what it was, and there was this young girl—only been wed a few weeks. She was standing outside her room, crying her eyes out. She was holding a baking tin, with a most revolting object sitting in the middle . . . (*She laughs at the memory*)

Tottie What was it?

Gran A rabbit, she was cooking for her man's meal. She had never cooked one before, and hadn't realized that you had to skin it first!

They laugh together

Wyn enters from the hall, interrupting the laughter. She still limps, but there is an air of alertness about her, and she is tidier

Tottie Have you heard from Edna?

Wyn I had a message. There are one or two women coming over. I don't know who they are, and they've got to wait their opportunity. There's a fight building up in Main Street, and the soldiers are trying to drive a wedge in the middle.

Gran Poor little devils. Some of them aren't old enough to have faced living, let alone dying.

Wyn Edna was fine, don't worry. It took a lot of courage to make that move, but she's glad that she did. She'll be along as soon as she's helped Franz shutter up the shop. He had his windows blasted last night, and some of the locals used it as a self-service—without payment!

Tottie Damn their hides. He's worked hard to keep that little place going, and there's many a woman been grateful, especially if she'd got a family to feed.

Gran With the city in this state, I suppose looting's the only entertainment they know.

Tottie Do you really think we shall do any good with this meeting? Where will we start—what do we say?

Wyn We start at the beginning—now—we must forget the past, otherwise we shall spend all night talking in circles.

There is a tap on the window—a distinct signal. Tottie starts to move, but Wyn stops her. The signal is repeated

Wyn goes out to the hall to open the front door.
Three women enter: they are Mary White, her sister-in-law Celia, and her mother-in-law Ellen. Ellen is middle-aged, bigoted, with a sharp temper, and tongue to match. Mary is younger; gentle-natured and thoughtful. Celia, Ellen's younger daughter, is intelligent and peaceful by nature. Wyn follows them in

There is a general air of wariness, but Gran goes on stitching

Tottie Come and sit you down. I'll see if the kettle's boiling.

Tottie goes towards the kitchen, but Ellen produces a gun and speaks quickly

Ellen Stay where you are. (*She crosses to the kitchen and looks round*)

Gran You can put that away, Ellen White. That's not needed here.

Ellen There's no harm in making sure.

Gran My Ted *saved* your life once—when you fell in the canal. We're hardly likely to take it now. See to the kettle, Tottie. I can do with a drink even if no-one else does.

Ellen We haven't come here on a social visit. Let's say what's to be said and get it over.

Gran That's a nice friendly tone to adopt, I must say.

Wyn Now, Gran, stop it. There's too much at stake. We must agree first on a common aim—to do what we can to get a truce.

Ellen On certain conditions.

Wyn Then you may as well go back and we'll forget that we ever met.

Ellen But you don't expect us to agree with what you propose without any concessions, any changes in attitude?

Wyn We must concern ourselves with one issue only—our wish to stop the fighting. The political and social battle can be argued round a table—what we've got to do is get our men round that table.

Mary Some of us haven't got our men alive to talk round a table —some didn't have a chance.

Wyn We've all got blood on our hands—we can't wash it off.

The sound of the fight grows louder and there is a sound of running feet approaching

Ellen The fight's spreading this way—we shouldn't have come.

Gran If you stay you'll do more good than going out there. It's peace you're seeking after all.

Ellen At any price?

Gran It's the cost of life you want to worry about.

Mary We've all paid enough. We must do something—the men won't. But we need the rest of the women behind us.

Wyn We could make a start by refusing to make any more petrol bombs, hide ammunition—and the agitators who hide from the police—and delight in stirring trouble wherever they go.

Ellen Do you think that it is going to be that easy? Just stopping? There'll be hell to pay when the men hear of it.

Tottie It's not exactly heaven now. It's their lives at stake as well as ours.

Celia That argument won't wash—they've got to the stage when they would rather die than give in.

Wyn Our men are equally determined, make no mistake about that—and many of the women, too . . .

Celia If we can't agree among ourselves we may as well give in.

Mary I've no man now, but I've got a child—fast growing— but into what? He must have forgotten the day when his father used to take him to the park, or watch a football match. He's never indoors, at home, except for his meals and his bed. The street's his playground now, and stone-throwing his favourite pastime.

Ellen He's a good boy.

Mary Is he? I don't know, but if we can't convince the men of the need of peace for the sake of the kids, then we're a poor lot.

Gran That makes sense.

Wyn We need to show our purpose—all together in one place. We need to do that quickly.

Celia It depends how soon we can make our contacts—and strengthen them.

Wyn That's important, to strengthen them. A vital message could pass like a flash through this town—and other places would follow our lead.

Wyn Can we at least agree to that? That we make our contacts, test reactions, and then agree to a further meeting? That's as far as we can go for now.

Gran It's a start. It's like this patch—the trousers aren't all that strong, but the patch will hold them together and give 'em a new lease of life, till we can afford new ones. Make do and mend—that's always been women's work.

The noise outside builds again. There is a sound of a woman scream-ing and banging on the front door. Tottie goes and opens it

Edna falls into the room. She is a sorry sight, covered in paint and rubbish, her hair shorn, her clothes tattered and ripped. She is sobbing hysterically

There is a general gasp of horror

Tottie (*kneeling by Edna*) Oh! My God!

Wyn Who the hell did this?

Gran Get her to the sofa.

Tottie I'll murder whoever is responsible for this.

Gran No. You won't. Get her cleaned up . . . that's the first thing.

Gran exits to the kitchen

Tottie cuddles Edna, becoming stained with the paint and dirt

Tottie She never hurt a soul. (*With a sudden thought, turning on Ellen*) It was because she went over to you as our contact. It was those bitches—your friends . . . (*She goes to attack Ellen*)

Ellen draws the gun, but this is knocked out of her hand by Mary, while Tottie is held back by Wyn

Mary There'll be no shooting here. It'll solve nothing.
Tottie My girl—look at my girl. (*She sits crying beside Edna*)

Gran returns from the kitchen with a drop of brandy

Gran Drink this, love—it'll do you good.
Edna (*with difficulty*) Don't fight, Mum. Don't fight.
Wyn Who did this, Edna. Was it the Blues?
Edna No—no . . .
Ellen You see—and you call us bitches. You class us all alike. You'd better look at your own folk.
Wyn Don't talk rot. Edna's known to us all—we wouldn't do this—she's been too much of a fighter for the cause.
Ellen She was keen enough to come over with an olive branch. Perhaps someone objected—or maybe she's been visiting the soldiers with messages of peace and love—of a kind!
Tottie You cow . . .
Gran Why don't you use your energy for something useful? You started to talk sense a few minutes ago, and now listen to you. You're as blind as a bats. Come on, Tottie, we'll get her up to the bathroom. Wyn, you get as much turps or paraffin that you can find in the shed. There's a can of it—and some in the old oil heater. Bring the scissors and a load of old newspapers —and the rest of that old sheet. Come on, Edna.

Tottie and Gran help Edna out of the room

Wyn starts to collect up newspapers, etc.

Celia This is so cruel—she'll remember it for the rest of her life.
Mary And she thought she was moving towards peace . . .
Ellen I still reckon she's been mixing with the khaki boys.
Wyn Not Edna. She's too fond of Franz and her boys—she's not the type.
Ellen Some women have only got to see the sparkle in a man's eye, and they're away—and not fussy where the man comes from.
Celia There's good and bad on all sides, Mum.

Ellen No doubt, but I don't want to know. At least the Reds are our blood, though they've polluted it a bit! The soldiers are different—different race—some of them a different colour. As far as I'm concerned, the only good soldier is a dead one. I'd tar and feather a daughter of mine if I caught her mixing with them . . .

Wyn Then you'd better start plucking. (*She looks at Celia*)

Ellen Plucking?

Wyn Yes. The first chicken you see—and a few more. You'll need plenty, and I shouldn't use tar. I'd use paint, you just tip the paint tin upside down—it's easier.

Ellen What the hell are you talking about?

Wyn You'd better ask Celia. She's your daughter.

Wyn exits to the kitchen

Ellen (*calling after her*) If you're insinuating that she's one of the whores that hang around the army camp, you're wrong. She knows that I'd beat the living daylights out of her.

Mary And a fat lot of good that would do. You're so bigoted, you don't want to see sense any more.

Ellen Celia?

Mary It's the best chance you've got, Celia—she's got to know sometime.

Ellen Know what? You've been carrying on with one of them— you slut. (*She slaps Celia's face*)

Celia Carrying on! I knew that you'd say that. That's the first thing that comes into your head—sex!

Ellen What else would those bastards want when they're away from home?

Mary (*quietly*) Comfort—a little peace, maybe.

Ellen Peace! That's ripe. They don't give us much peace with their patrols, and their tanks rumbling through the streets day and night.

Celia They didn't ask to come here. They're trying to stop us killing ourselves and everyone else in sight.

Ellen We had a cause—it's none of their business.

Mary They should have left us in our own mess, I suppose.

Celia Mum, I didn't mean it to happen this way—it all started as a joke, really.

Mary But it's serious now, isn't it?

Celia Mum. After Chrissie Brown got raped, I used to go and sit with her . . .

Ellen starts to interrupt

Yes, I know, but she was my friend at school. I couldn't think of her as an enemy of mine. It upset me seeing her like that—giggling one minute, crying the next and sometimes screaming. When I left her, I couldn't come home and tell you where I'd been. I used to walk out of town and try to get away from the noise and mess of the streets. It was as if I needed some fresh air to blow the dirt from my mind—the thought of Chrissie, and what had happened to her. She had always been such a lovely girl—so happy.

Ellen Men—I'd castrate the lot of them . . .

Mary You wouldn't if you had lost your man as I have.

Ellen We're not talking about you and Tom . . .

Mary In his loving there was tenderness—yes, and joy for me too. He was your son. Would you call him a beast?

Ellen You were lucky.

Mary And you were not—and it's coloured your judgement of all men. I felt the bitterness the first time I entered your house. Tom's Dad never knew a soft smile or a kind word. You begrudged him his loving as if it were obscene.

Ellen It wasn't your business—you don't know half of it.

Mary No—but I could guess.

Ellen I don't want to talk about that.

Mary You should. Your generation felt that it was better to create frustration and bitterness, under a cloak called decency.

Ellen We kept our respectability——

Celia —and your skeletons in the cupboard.

Ellen I never became a fancy woman for any man.

Celia I'm not Brian's fancy woman—not in the way you mean. My love for him is special. He wanted a little peace and quiet, like me, and when he wasn't on patrol he just walked away from the noisy streets. So many parts of the city are out of bounds any rate.

Ellen (*bitterly*) They shouldn't be here—they're not wanted.

Celia (*shouting*) Don't you ever listen? Brian is a quiet boy. (*She is calmer now*) He just wanted the freedom of the fields—

we met—talked—met again—and fell in love. There's no
harm in him—he's just doing a job of work—and he's hating
every minute of it.

Ellen Then he shouldn't have joined the Army.

Mary I don't suppose he ever envisaged being in this situation;
fighting a common enemy is one thing, but acting as a strong-
armed police force is another.

Celia He was out of work, Mum. Made redundant after three
years' apprenticeship and two years' employment. The shipyard
closed and the Army was the only career left. Their country
knows unemployment and poverty, too, you know. We're not
the only sufferers.

Ellen And what kind of future do you see for yourself with him?

Celia We're not going to stay here. We're going to emigrate.
We're sick to death of being called "Blues", "Reds", "this"
or "that". We're going to find a new label.

Ellen You'll never go.

Mary It's the best thing for them—to get away from this mad-
house.

Ellen It's her home!

Celia Home? It's never been that. It's always been a bloody
battlefield of one sort or another—private wars, family feuds,
and now civil war. Brian and I want to get out—right out—
and we're going at the first opportunity—if we live that long
in this hell hole.

Ellen You'd leave us in it, and wouldn't care a damn.

Celia I do care. That's why I'm here tonight. I'll clutch at any
straw that gives a hope of sanity. I thought that's what we all
came here for tonight—and so far we've done nothing but
fight and argue.

Ellen What did you expect? I didn't bargain for this. Your dad
will kill you when he finds out.

Mary No, he won't—not if you tell him with love. Give him
time to get used to the idea. Give Celia time to get away. Let
her see things in perspective. Maybe if she and the boy are
separated for awhile they won't be so keen.

Celia (*fiercely*) We'll love the more.

Ellen (*suddenly tired*) We'll see. We'll see. Come on home.
There's nothing to wait for here.

Mary But the others?

Ellen We've got enough on our plate—and so have they . . .
They move towards the hall door

Gran enters from the stairs

Gran You're off then?
Ellen No point in stopping.
Gran I wouldn't say that.
Mary How's Edna?
Gran She'll be all right. We're a tough lot. If you're going, you
   might remember what's been said, and see what can be done?
Ellen We've got other problems.
Gran Do you know who attacked Edna? It was children—
   children, not yet out of their teens.
Mary (*sitting with fear*) Children?
Gran There was a gang of them—girls as well as boys. They'd
   been throwing stones at the soldiers. Edna noticed that they'd
   got some of the things that had been looted from Franz's
   shop. She was so angry that she lashed out at them—with her
   tongue—that's all, but they turned on her—like a pack. One
   of them got hold of a can of paint, God knows from where,
   and after they'd beaten her to the ground, they just tipped it
   over her, rolled her in the dirt and rubble, and hacked at her
   hair with penknives.
Ellen I don't believe it . . . whose children were they?
Mary Does it matter? The fact that any youngster could con-
   template such an act, and to a woman at that—it's horrible.
Celia What do you expect, in a place where the adults have gone
   mad?
Ellen It's the parents. They've got no control—no discipline.
Mary You try bringing up a boy of eleven in this place, and see
   if you can control him—especially with no husband to help
   you.
Ellen Our Tommy's a good lad.
Celia I was a "good" girl till you found out I'd fallen in love
   with a foreign soldier.
Mary The kids can't see a paper, hear the radio, see the tele,
   without seeing violence somewhere—and here they live with
   it—day and night.

Celia And you expect them to know the difference between right and wrong? There's little hope of that . . .

Gran But, my God, we've got to cling to that little hope—otherwise we're sunk.

Mary Clinging's not enough. We've got to do.

Celia But what? Do what? It's so easy to say.

Mary God knows. I'm so tired I don't know where to start.

Ellen Come on. Let's go home—it's been a wearing evening—one we won't forget in a hurry . . .

Celia But we'll talk about it . . .

Gran You do just that—keep talking—you might find the answer one day.

The visitors go

Gran sits by the fire. She picks up the trousers and renews the sewing, as the sound of strife continues, and—

the CURTAIN *falls*

FURNITURE AND PROPERTY LIST

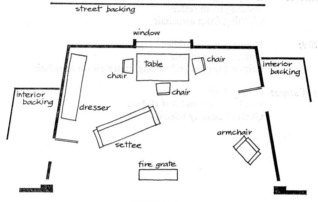

SCENE 1

On stage: Settee. *On it:* rumpled bedding, newspapers, general untidiness

Armchair. *Over back:* clothing, including **Gran**'s coat

3 small chairs

Dresser

Table. *On it:* cloth, remains of hasty meal, plates, cups, saucers, knives, forks, teaspoons, sugar bowl

On window: shutters, boarding to cover broken glass, torn curtains

Down C: firegrate, fender, poker

Around room generally: newspapers, magazines, various untidy oddments

Carpet

Off stage: Bottle of milk (**Gran**)

Milk jug (**Edna**)

Bowl of water (**Tottie**)

Sheeting and scissors (**Tottie**)

Personal: **Edna:** bandage

SCENE 2

Strike: Everything from table except cloth
                Bedding from settee
                Clothing from armchair

Set: Room generally tidier
                Shutters on window
                Pair of trousers and sewing materials on armchair

Off stage: Gun (**Ellen**)
                Bowl of stain and dirt (**Edna**)
                Glass of brandy (**Gran**)

LIGHTING PLOT

Property fittings required: pendant, coal fire glow effect
Interior. A living-room

SCENE 1. Early morning

To open: Dim light filtering through shutters

Cue 1	**Gran** removes shutters *Bring up general lighting to early morning*	(Page 1)
Cue 2	**Edna** pokes fire *Bring up red glow down* C	(Page 2)
Cue 3	**Tottie:** ". . . to be done by someone" *Fade to Black-Out*	(Page 9)

SCENE 2. Evening

To open: Black-Out

Cue 4	At opening of scene *Fade up to interior lighting: pendant on*	(Page 9)

EFFECTS PLOT

SCENE 1

Cue 1   AS CURTAIN rises   (Page 1)

Sounds of broken glass being swept up and other after-battle noises. Continue spasmodically through Scene

SCENE 2

Cue 2   **Tottie:** "... than breaking them"   (Page 9)

Pause—then burst of gunfire. Intermittent sounds of strife continue throughout scene

Cue 3   **Gran:** "... always been women's work"   (Page 14)

Sounds of fighting and turmoil in street

Music to open and close play and cover time lapse: "Mars—God of War" from *The Planet Suite* by Holst.